THE CATASTROPHES

poems by

Marie Scarles

Finishing Line Press
Georgetown, Kentucky

The starting-point of critical elaboration is the consciousness of what one really is, and is "knowing thyself" as a product of the historical processes to date, which has deposited in you an infinity of traces without leaving an inventory.
—Antonio Gramsci

Every poem is an effort at ceremony.
I asked for a way in.
—Joy Harjo

THE CATASTROPHES

For those who remember and resist

ACKNOWLEDGMENTS

Earlier versions of these poems were published in the following journals:

"Fireflies" in *Tiger Moth Review*
"Nature (n.)" in *Thimble Magazine*
"Pipeline" and "Mother/Nature" in *About Place Journal*
"After the Flood, You Will Know Our True Names" in *Sundog Lit*

Publisher: Leah Huete de Maines
Editor: Christen Kincaid
Cover Art: Marie Scarles
Author Photo: Maxwell Linton
Cover Design: Elizabeth Maines McCleavy

Order online: www.finishinglinepress.com
Also available on amazon.com

Author inquiries and mail orders:
Finishing Line Press
PO Box 1626
Georgetown, Kentucky 40324
USA

Contents

Monocrop: Connecticut River Valley

Each vinyl-sided home that dots the development's
slide of cement stands quiet, each driveway paved

at a slope reaches down for the road.
I pace the sidewalk looking for something to hold,

find only a fleet of SUVs—white shells gleaming.
What makes a place feel like home? A student asked in class

& together we parsed what it means to belong.
I couldn't tell him. I don't know how to sense the cardinal

directions in this valley, can't name the plants that perfume
the densest days of June. I do know the blacktop

warms my bare soles when I go walking,
sleepless, after midnight, and the distant chirp

of frogs over an AC unit's growl.
I know the feeling, in this valley, of being

far from home, though it's the only place
I've called my own. Tell me: who isn't a stranger.

Connecticut's Last Commercial Fishing Port

Small boats rest against their pilings. Inlet stilled by fog. Weathered clapboard houses line the shore. A Christmas tree out of lobster traps, a stacked pyramid of painted buoys tied to wire boughs. In the square beside the library, no one sits or runs. A local woman tells me the traps cost $50,000. Who here remembers this port at its peak? The catch coming in daily, fish ice-packed in crates, piled for delivery? In a storefront window, I see me as I feel: urban, out of place, wool coat buttoned at the waist, weathered leather boots. As a child, I felt displaced. Before my mother died, she took me to this very square. We bought fresh bread and local vegetables. She wore her wool cinched at the hip and boots of worn black leather. A town's memory lasts for generations. This one harbors whaling ships, captains and their families on the coast. It holds its first inhabitants, the Pequot and the Narragansett, who fished its marshes and built fires along the river. I walk across the playground, past the swings where villages once stood. *The state's last commercial fishing port*, she tells me, leaning close.

Nature

noun | na - ture | 'nā-chər

      a : humankind's original or natural condition
      b : a simplified mode of life resembling this condition

This language takes tautology as definition. Nature = a natural condition for mankind. [Sic] the whole statement. The language our land's laws rest on is empty.

When Europeans arrived, North America was "legally" empty. How? A "savage" race of men— people of the sauvage, or forest—didn't cultivate the land with their own labor; merely *used the fruits.*

[Sic] the whole statement.

Settler's "providence" = the new world formed for settlement by a God, beneficent. Left alone (with Others) it was disorderly, useless wilderness. But how to [sic] it all, in thought, action, and language?

*

If only it were that easy to edit history, as if on a page. "What did literature ever do for you?" asks clickbait, and I think of a question posed by an essay I can no longer find online: Does literature's personal testimony leave you alone with your grief, or does it tie you to something wider, something larger, something other than you, pronoun, bound down and alone?

*

As if your life depended on it—wrote Adrienne Rich of writing.

"I don't like her strident tone" a student told me after we read this. "It seems like she just wants to tell you what to do."

*

The flowers whisper: the violet morning glories of summer, fat trumpets on their vines, have withered out. Had I not faced them from my desk at the window, would I have heard their murmur? Poetry is a way of reading, a poet once told me.

I am learning how to hear what's on the page, behind the words, behind the rage. To ask who lives on what land, and what binds the paper's wood and fiber, and what hands hold what bundles of ink and glue, which lithium batteries or plastic bags. A theory: Poetry teaches you not how to speak, but how to listen.

Fireflies
Catastrophe of the Field

Before the music starts in Prospect Park
I watch fireflies flicker & glow.
Around me, the air smells of honeysuckle
& petrochemical. And the field?

Ten stops out on the train, the parks grow
tenements. A migrant family sleeps
in an airless room, head-to-toe, no sheets.
A woman's eyes look back at me

from my phone's rolling screen
her image sold on an object made
by workers poisoned with mercury. I see trees
snapped to twigs by hailstorms & kids

split from their parents, fingers laced
in the bars of a cage. Scientists say we've entered
the age of plastics—headlines flicker
between C-list celebrities. A critic praises

a book of poems I am reading:
"there's no hint of a social agenda"
and I see the fireflies glowing.
They hover over the field, their brilliance

derived from an enzyme—*luciferase*—yes,
from the Latin one: lucifer—
bringer of light. My phone screen
brings light, divides night into shards

of day. In the dark of the bandshell, I raise
my lit screen, wave it and sway.
But why do I keep swaying and singing?
There's so little left to say.

Brownfield

Catastrophe of the Shale

They preside over the brownfield, refineries
sketched on the horizon, silhouettes against the sable

sky. I've come here on my way from somewhere else
alone, through rusted scenery. It is not beauty

that fuels me. I stop for gas
& sour coffee & read about the town I've crossed through.

In the towns around the drills, girls
go missing. Some men, after months on oil rigs, turn

their own exhaustion on their wives. What a man
cannot master

masters him. Spills onto people
he can reach. When my father was a child,

his hit him with belts. That's just how it was then,
he tells me. Me, I punished my teddy—stuffed him

in the plastic toy oven.
That's all there is to it: Fear begets fear.

Under the bright lights of a boardroom, two men
clasp hands and shake. All spills begin upstream, the bottom

line throbbing. The line that breaks a man or woman
is mere runoff, the horizon, a flood of groundwater scum.

The horizon is a place where women
go missing. As if missing were a place to which one could run.

Everyday Disaster
Commute as Catastrophe

Mine are the hours on the train, body pressed
against another woman, a man and a man. The in-
coat sweat. Urge, burning, from bladder to back.
Glass in the whites of my eyes, nights of dry panic—
heat heaving across my chest. Mine are the sirens
spinning below my open window, the robbery in the deli downstairs.
Mine is the caution tape, and the person who lies
there, unwilling. Mine is my own body in the street,
and—*hey you look good today*—the man
who grabs my hand on my way to the train. Mine.
Mine is the ten minutes
another man follows me. Mine the minute clinic I hide in, while he waits
in the park behind a tree, like some cartoon villain,
his stick legs tip-toeing around the trunk.
And mine is yet another man who stalks me across six blocks—
BITCH LOOK AT ME WHEN I'M TALKING TO YOU—
changing sides to keep me in his sight-line.
Mine the sun pinning me to the concrete. Boiled and skinless,
I pull my body through the streets. My pelvis is searing,
my joints are aflame. Mine is the film of sweat
in the crook of my elbow. Stench of my fear, and my shame.

Ecotone: Southeastern Connecticut

But if it doesn't smell of the earth, it isn't good for the earth.
—Adrienne Rich

On the southbound train, scenes of abandonment :: weeds
jutting grassy heads through gravel

an empty lot filled with tires, iron bars, refrigerators
rust-devoured corrugated tin

energy transfer-stations tangled with live wires, tubes
magnetic, electric & toxic :: each passing scene

*

Today you will experience the supernatural grace of compassion
say the stars in their app, sidereal and digital

the Thames River sucks on motor homes tucked
against the bank, about to tip into the water we cross over ::

a hush between the tracks and brick face of a crumbling factory
its windows shattered, walls scribbled on, thick-lettered

graffiti the colors of blood, indigo & ivory
while beside it, abandoned vans strangled in the reeds

& row houses shuttered on the hill, paint
chipping, roofs collapsing

the whole block leaning to the right

*

At the dead-end of opportunity
between land, man, & industry :: comes memory

a boy from school who cracked his teeth on concrete
(his family couldn't pay to fix them for weeks)

a boy who clawed at my butt under my skirt & one
whose scrawled handwriting struggled   the curves of an S or C

in boyhood, adolescence, what rushes in
to fill the gaps in a boy's vulnerability?

Power over girls, or guns that hang low
                    & heavy from the trees

he grabs the closest weapon he can reach

*

Down the coast, a thread of facilities weaves ::
                    weapons manufacturing & a deepwater harbor
a fleet of submarines

shards pass me in the scenery

city that builds helicopters for the military
                    & the Long Island Sound, where New Yorkers go sailing

*

As a teen, I watched the boys
                    slugging whiskey & Yuengling,
                              then heroin & speed, blaming

"Mexicans"   "the Middle East"
repeating the keywords, their fathers

                    :: weapons, chemicals, army
                    prisons or police

                              they held the faith—
                              work hard & do anything—

*

I remember the smell

        (the burnt edges of the dream)

I left
I closed the door

(I tried not to breathe)

*

From the train's window seat, I look east   toward a graveyard of wrecked
cars

      grasses sprout in the trash heaps

            a concrete lot for rusty boats & RVs

To the west, white masts dot the blue sea

               Between the scenes I cannot be cleaved from,

them :: those who carry the weapons

            those who built the tracks

*

      On the southbound train, trees flicker

            asters sprout wild between the freeway's aisles

& history runs under the rumble of thunderclouds & ATVs

      in shades of umber, oak, & green

Mystic, Connecticut

During the Mystic Massacre of 1637, between 400 and 700 Pequot men, women, and children were murdered or abducted when English colonists set fire to the Pequot Fort near the Mystic River. The Mystic Massacre played a decisive role in shaping colonial and U.S. policy toward Native Americans.

This morning in Mystic, loafered tourists
flock in from nearby towns while
across the past's

vast valley, blistered women
stumble from fires. My mother,
twenty-eight, follows her husband

downtown, toward the estuary,
across the drawbridge with its
massive bascules

hanging heavy over
the sweet-shops like a threat.
She'd like to linger mid-

way across the bridge, to
take in the white sails and
black waters

but her husband is late,
his job interview waits.
It was like a dream,

she told me decades later.
We couldn't believe
we'd moved to a place

with such beauty. But beauty
hides as much as it reveals.
What came of them.

The women, children,
bodies hurled into
the river's mouth?

Beneath the glinting
waters lie sand-
like granules of bone.

Ongoing Colony

strip mall parking lot driveways
                              weeds jut through cracked rock

parched lawns
            doves on the interstate guard rail, cooing

                                    here ::
                                    nuclear power plant
here ::
correctional facility
                        :: empty industrial town
                              two front teeth, missing

concrete ecology of big-box stores &
frozen TV dinners

            :: ache of the 12-hour day   at the refinery
                        penitentiary   factory

downhill from the great stone library ::
historic homes with anchored placards to mark the years they were built
                              —1896, 1907, 1912—

                  between buildings   cobbled alleys
                  & cottages painted the colors of daybreak's pastel face

—over the river   a drawbridge at the center—

                  solid concrete blocks & lattice of steel
                              ready to tilt back

                  let a yacht pass through the river's neck
                              past the bar and me in it

                              serving rare steak
red liquid leaks across white plates

My Colony

at fifteen I'd climb the cliffside behind the former factory,

        skirt its brick ledge and sit, feet dangling
over the water, over the boats

        carving wakes in and out of the river's mouth

between road and house, parking lot and park, it was

a place from which to watch:
        I wafted above the briny river like a scent

            my solitude clean as a rock

Country Club Waitress, Age Nineteen

In my button-down and nylon slacks,
I sat out back at the end of the 9-hole course,
pants stuck to my thighs in the heat, the mist
of sprinklers coming on. Dusk was just
beginning to tint the sky purple, polo pink.
In my 10-minute break as the golfers ate, I watched
the bartender, her calves tattooed with
thick-petaled irises, pace the parking lot,
smoke trailing in her wake. With each step
the flowers trembled. Hunched exhausted
on the curb, I held a paper plate of leftovers
—cold strip-steak, green beans, mashed potatoes—
and ached with a relief so deep
I could ride it out over the golf course, past
the stables, past tobacco farms with tractors
tucked in barns, out toward the quarry
where a high-school classmate dove off the cliff,
where another crashed on a country road at dawn.
But because what cannot be run from must be
endured, the manager called my name.
I rose, tied on my apron and stepped back
across the asphalt, past the lawn, into the kitchen,
where I hoisted up my giant plastic tray
to collect the diners' soiled plates.

Pipeline

Catastrophe of Extraction

Every morning grays the same. I bring my body
to the kitchen window, stare past the bamboo reeds, past
the neighbor's chain-link fence, past the power lines,
the fat squirrels, the red bricks of the Victorians with
wide window-booths, out toward the tracks that seam
over Baltimore and Spruce, past the highway's spiral curls,
around the museum, past the Schuylkill, its steady bleat
against the land's flanks, past those boxy houses tucked in tight,
to the end of what my mind's eye sees:

Plumes rise there, from the refinery, its campus
of concrete and rust. Each morning, I lie in bed and listen
to my love's shallow breath, afraid of air that makes him gasp
himself awake. Every morning I haul my body up
and stand at the range, boiling coffee, plating eggs.
Plate, coffee, air, eggs: I survive on a filthy line. I breathe
what once seethed under the crust, and then—piped up—
I hold my cup.

Here Comes the Future
Corporate Catastrophe

~~In which no one~~
~~will be held~~
~~ACCOUNTABLE~~
~~for the billion-billion~~
~~little deaths.~~

~~In which we~~
~~will make a killing,~~
~~a marker of EXCELLENCE,~~
~~INNOVATION—~~
~~this bulldozed field~~
~~one among many~~
~~SMART SOLUTIONS,~~
~~allowing STAKEHOLDERS~~
~~to recoup their SHARE.~~

~~When it comes, they will welcome us,~~
~~warehouse workers, servers, drivers, nurses,~~
~~to the true MERITOCRACY:~~
~~we, the RESILIENT HUMAN CAPITAL,~~
~~who will no longer cry ourselves~~
~~to sleep at night, but PIVOT~~
~~from FAILURE toward~~
~~FLEXIBILITY, then FREEDOM.~~

~~Then we too will be~~
~~EMPOWERED.~~

FREE
of every other

Side Effects
Another Corporate Catastrophe

Include your doctor, hands folded, who told you, "I'm sorry"
Include mine telling me, "It's hard to live with; there's not much we can do"
Include the statements *the body changes as you age & it's stress-induced*
Include the fact that change is not the same as pain & your body growing
       thinner by the day
Include nausea, headache, hair loss, bleeding, & a pain that comes from the
       bone
Include blood clots, cancer, stroke
Include the doctor who sent me home with pills to mask my pain & an
       endless prescription
Include no diagnosis & that those capsules ravaged my stomach, organs,
       moods &
Include no warning of what was to come
Include the word "sorry," which is not sufficient
Include harm, unevenly distributed, & that the nearby refinery scores
       highest in the nation for
       benzene fumes
Include tap water with contaminants
"Legal" does not equal "safe"
Include my speculations that there is no such thing as safety & they would
       privatize the water
       & they did
       & it poisoned men, women, & children
       & children now live or die from "elevated" levels of lead
Include women's bodies, our first environment, absorbing toxins that settle
       into fat & skin & bones
Include children
       & include land, stolen
       & land, which is the common ground for all radical action
       & the factories, at which my grandparents worked, ate, & drank
       & the neighborhood that they called home, named after the ozone
       & include you, who smoothed my hair & told me, *Take care of your*
          father & brother for me &
Include your advice: *Never rely on a man for cash*
Include your life & your life ending
       & the doctors who told you to "drink water" & "eat greens"
       & the drug that saved, then killed you
Your death itself was a side effect
       & so, include medicine and intention

Include effects
       & include the drug company's web menu with its INVESTOR
              RELATIONS & STOCK EXCHANGE
       & the company's worth (one hundred billion) today
       & you who wanted to shape your own life & its labors
       & poesis, or how I make mine
Include our rights & other lies
       & the fact that I can find no answer to the question of why you died
Include the historical processes to date, which have deposited in you *an*
       infinity of traces without leaving an inventory & that therefore *it is*
       imperative at the outset to compile such an inventory
Include this poem, taking stock, taking focus, setting its gaze—ready to
       aim—ready to fire—
And include pain, in which I too become dangerous

When Every Hour Needs Too Much and Gives Too Little Back
Little Catastrophes

At four, before the patrons arrive,
the bar's wood-paneled walls pulse.
Stacked glasses shine
in towers two rows tall.
By seven, they'll be scattered
over tables like what
you don't know. Sweat under
your apron's arms grows long
across your shirt. Nine o'clock, ten,
and the dinner crowd gives up
to a rush of drinkers clustered
in the bar's backyard: dark denim,
tight dresses, a dash of shimmer on lids
and you: serving a second gin martini, up,
your face unremarkable, creased and
dimly smiling. Midnight arrives, and you break
in the alley beside the dumpsters
rank with grease and table scraps to smoke
a cigarette you neither need nor enjoy,
just to stand under the stars
for two minutes and feel the night-work
vibrate in your soles. The longest hours
are still to come: the final order, a man
who will not leave the bar's black lip,
bloated face keening, the mop,
the bleach, toilets and tables,
and then dawn's dark pedaling
toward home, weak light through
curtains of your basement bedroom—
watered-down whiskey abandoned
on a worn table. Your hands,
which wiped it dozens of days in a row.
Only then will you step forward
of your own accord, replying solely to
your body's call, and within the blue-tiled stall
let cool water run over your eyes, your mouth,
your waning hours, the only ones in which
you don't feel so alone.

The Flood
Catastrophe Prototype

The downtown highway floods with
      brown water, sewage—
and a friend
      tells me about a Wendy's employee,
stranded and then
      rescued from the liquid belly
of the store via helicopter.
      I read about a woman trapped
in her garden apartment,
      windows shattering
inward from the small yard
      where she'd planted marigolds
the color of autumns
      in Vermont. To reporters
her neighbors testified:
      We tried—
we heard her cry,
      but the waters came
too fast, too strong.
      Too fast, too strong
this transition, these burning hills
      turned to clouds of dust and char.
The last I read,
      our debts to land and air and water
cannot be paid off.
      To the living world, Earth—
we owe it all, our debt,
      bad credit. Man made
the disaster we cannot
      not try to stop.

3,000 Miles from the Oil War
Catastrophe Seen from Afar

She stands over blanketed earth, a ball field at the heart
of empire. The pixelated sky glitters into crystals, her chest

plundering her mind. Black ice still silvers the parking lot's
straight white lines. It cannot call itself a war without

equal and opposite force. The night above holds cold,
clear and dark. When she conjures the dead,

it's like tracing the hollow barrel of a tank's front-loaded gun.
She needles like ice. Distance does not numb.

Mother/Nature

I don't remember learning how to pray, only trying to,
kneeling in a fiction I did not design

Hardwood under downy knees
what would come I could not say

soft dark of the bedroom
light under the door illuminating the woodgrain

I feigned feeling humility, a kind of child's play,
and tried repentance on for size to see how it suited me

My mother sensed something under the god-talk
and repetition of liturgy

in the dark of a chapel by the sea she praised St. Mary
God is love, she told me   *God is what I want him to be*

*

Through a distance of years & miles, I walk the Woodlands Cemetery
to feel under my feet the hot dirt of midsummer

here where train tracks pass over marsh banks
so naturally, reeds part for them

From above, even the river is pocked by crop circles,
channels of blue-brown in the marsh body like arteries

algae blooms over the surface: a sign of nutrient profusion
a decay that feeds the green and robs the fish of oxygen they need

to breathe   The way she struggled at the end, tubes running oxygen to
her chest—

Rest now, her doctor told her. *Lia, you can rest.*

*

Heavy air settles over the cemetery, thunderclouds build columns of steam
& the sweet vanilla smell of some common shrub blooming

grasslands on the water   small islands of trees
white clouds hang over the river's deep green

In the midmorning of my life, it feels unnatural
to be here   to be here without her

Flatbush, After Pain

the light shifts over the row houses first
a dawn-tinted rose, then with the white-blue sky over
square windows

the schoolyard is quiet; still,
sparrows voice the day-start

and the raw ragged edges of potholes make like great gnashing teeth
their marks in the road, but they're no threat, not
at this hour, not yet

the Q train is vibrating in the distance
& at the depot, where a driver prepares for the next shift, slinging
a lunchbox over the back of her seat—

the day grows gold, and the storefronts roll up their grates like great eyes
opening; the florist is preparing a spray of spring greens and sprigs of white
and violet buds for display—

the prep cook at corner diner chops, smooth and sure, a quart of red onions
and a girl stirs dried black tea leaves in a cup of scalding water;

by the lake, a woman walks the muddied path at the back
of the cemetery, and beside the railway and the water

beyond the fence, three men in neon caps survey the railway's iron lines
& the wooden ties binding them together

Gowanus Rising
Catastrophe of Industry

There was a scrapyard, a high-staired subway entrance, bare November sun glinting over the chrome body of the station, there was a putrid seam of sewage throbbing under the canal water, graffiti reminding us that RENT IS THEFT, and strung-out men and women keeling over two blocks from the methadone clinic, there was litter from the 9th Street Deli, paper coffee cups and plastic bottles and empty cigarette cartons, there was also a green-brown lot mulched over for native plants to grow—coastal bluestem and sea oats, bottlebrush grass, Cherokee sedge, white wood aster, creeping sedum, wild columbine, nodding onion and common yarrow—and, there was a tower of glass and a tower of iron and a tower of shining metal knives at midday, vast tract-like apartments with white-lit museum interiors, there was an estuary where Lenape villages once stood, with oysters the size of dinner plates, there was the oily sheen of coal tar waste, there were two buildings to house the public, three generations under one roof, sometimes there was sea air, there was blue and gray and yellow, the smell of ginkgo nuts crushed into the pavement, a rotting wind, urine sprayed in a wave on plywood construction barriers, there were the federal plans and the state plans and the city plans and the neighborhood's demands for a poison-free schoolyard, ignored, there was the blue jay—*cyanocitta cristata*—calling from the trees under the freeway, its territory lost in rising degrees, there was a truck depot for shipping and a cluster of 18-wheelers parked beside the artist lofts, there was a mannequin against the chain-link fence and me, pacing around the canal in my boots with an empty film roll, a jammed shutter and, leaving as I arrive, the voices of my parents rising to remind me *here, you can survive and thrive.*

The Road

Heavy heat swallows the thick trees I drive between.
        The clouds moving above me are gods, slumber-filled

with their own sorrows. The past bubbles up—
        a highway-side spring. I stay in my lane

heart thundering in its cage.
        I barely hear it at first, the rain

shuddering overhead like a hand-woven rug.
        It's all still there:

even with fresh cells
        my skin carries the trace of my parents' hands.

Water remembers. We are made of oceans bound into
        forms.   Walker, wrote Machado

There is no road,
        the road is made by walking. I like the truth of it,

but also the lie. The road on which I drive
        was laid right here, but could've been otherwise, which means

what is
        can always be revised.

*

I blink and it's September, my grandmother telling me
        of her pre-dawn walks nearly a century past:

she led goats into town, carrying pails for fresh milk
        squeezed from each udder at the villagers' doors.

Morning dwindles. The sun rises through beech leaves
        in her kitchen window, which looks out over a parking lot.

The middle is always approaching. It accumulates like skin cells
        that later slough off, and I will never find again

the selves they take with them. My eyes,
        becoming more like my father's.

*

We sculpt our lives—or they sculpt us.
        My smile grows lined, the sea heats

to half-boil. On my desk the spider plant shifts,
        glossy leaves following the light.

The low roar of a plane
        ascending over Brooklyn.

At Coney, the waves keep licking
        the sand where my grandmother picnicked.

History repeats, but I'm not there, not yet.
        The middle is still ahead,

the building's sidewalk lush with weeds.
        I love the largest:

six feet tall with a downy,
        thorny stalk and leaves the size of maps.

I take its portrait
        and the next time I pass, it's been chopped.

Its seeds will inherit this plot
        long after my building is gone—rancid
trash bags in the alley, rusted bicycles,
        the razor-headed fence. Tonight

the sky will turn violet over the granite
        library steps. The days are long, or long-enough.

Light lingers in the twilight air. Each evening
        I return to the same park trail

looking for shifts in the reeds, the ducks,
        the hunched night-herons. Yellow flowers unfurl

from water lilies,
        secret frogs beneath them. Music

rises over the man-made lake,
        note by note into the air.

Summer Night

long humid nights in summer   metal chair legs pressed into the tar-
    patched roof
we watched planes descend into LaGuardia & JFK   satellites
sailing down to earth   music from the street & frying meat
        & the sweet-foul smell of garbage drifting in whiffs

we pressed cold bottles against our chests as we talked, kissed,
descended to make a late-night dinner   spaghetti in cracked plastic
        bowls
& up to the roof again :: in that apartment   mold crawled through
the bathroom & a lone tree in the courtyard stood over the building's
army of bins   a plastic bag trapped in it   fluttered in sun and
    wind

weekends   after long shifts we rode our bikes on the path down
    Bedford through
Flatbush, Midwood,   down to the Rockaway's edge & after
touching the sea with our throats, our feet   after dunking our heads into
    the sea,
with salted hair and damp tees   in our bodies young and plain
we rode the subway home, clinging to the city's periphery

where our parents grew up like sidewalk weeds   in blood,
in spirit, we belong   in this city of mothers and grandmothers,
there is the textile factory where Nonna sewed knock-off bags & dresses
there's the salon where my aunt washed hair here's the laundromat where
    my cousins
played behind jackets coated in chemical film   & the yard of a pit
    bull they hid from

there's the lot where my mother grew figs & grapes in red clay pots
& the tin awning leaning over the concrete yard   here's the home my
    family bought after
Italy, after East New York,   where families took loans from banks
    that lent to
whites only

When I try to return to the scenes of their lives, it's to discover what made
    my long
sweet summer nights possible   in this city where money's bloody river
    rules

everything filled with light ::   skylines, planes, condos on the Sound

even the seeds of our young and ordinary lives
where we clink bottles on a hot tar roof in Brooklyn, sweating, surviving,
          wondering when   it will be time

Autogeography

As a girl, I climbed
        high into the backyard cedar,
sap & bark sticking to my palms.
        Some-THING there-IS
that-DOES not-LOVE a-WALL
        I learned in school
& I'd chant it, feet swinging
        in the cedar's long boughs.
Below me lay
        stone walls built by
by farmhands in the 18th century,
        farmhands who cleared the land
long before. Below those lines of stone
        that divided the land
into fractions, lay the bones of the laborers—
        indentured & enslaved—
who stacked stone
        over stone over stone.

*

In Ezekiel, the cedar's
        long arms were a symbol:
"spiritual and natural progress."
        Therefore his height was exalted
above all other trees of the *field,*
        and his boughs were multiplied,
and his branches became long
        of the multitude of waters.

*

I remember the daytime
        sound of crickets
as I built around me
        treehouse of branches,

a dream home in the sky,
        and something of the Bible quote
seems true. I felt it too,
        how height exalted me

& how the spirit shifted
        in the wind & cedar's crown.

*

In the forest
        around my childhood house
Pequot women
        planted corn & beans,
cut clearings in the trees,
        & tended vines of squash.
My mother planted
        peppers & zucchini
in our backyard plot,
        but woodchucks ate each vegetable
that sprouted.
        Below, the glacial stones
push up & out
        from the ground,
send rock walls tumbling
        to earth. I do not wish
to live above all other
        trees of the field,
or to drink from
        siphoned waters.
I see me as a child,
        swinging high up in the cedar.
I must begin again.
        I ask her to climb down.

After the Flood, You Will Know Our True Names

salt and oil
soft bread of the mouth
sonorous in friendship
campfire-haired freedom
full-petaled violet iris
girlhood daydream
autumn afternoon—reds browns golds greens
systematic erotics of evening
muscled wave, a people's movement
gray expanse of the Atlantic Pacific Indian Arctic
underwater world-making
dance dance dance dance dance
liberty of the duped & the damned
maybe magic, maybe fate
the queendom of heaven on dirt
one another's landbodies
what they steal from me they steal from you, your struggle is my own
the ecstasy of the present
redemption of the dance floor
burning ledgers, freed accountants
"food and drink, housing and clothing in adequate quality and quantity"
underminers of exploitation
blameless shameless immaculate heart
the superstructure of communal hand-holding
health in the hands of community
uncontrollable agents of the social
bewildered children of earth
so well, so well—so blessedly well
holistic economists of the heart
things in their surroundings
our plant- and animal-people
amateur creations
the little snail's trail
ongoing transformations
each according to ability and need
all of us with a real chance at living

Notes

The chapbook's epigraphs are drawn from Joy Harjo's poem "In Mystic," which inspired several of the poems about my hometown of Mystic, Connecticut, and Antonio Gramsci's *Prison Notebooks*.

The epigraph to "Ecotone" comes from Adrienne Rich's essay "Notes towards a Politics of Location."

The poem "Nature" draws from William Cronon's book *Changes in the Land: Indians, Colonists, and the Ecology of New England* and the Merriam-Webster Dictionary. It also quotes Adrienne Rich's essay "As If Your Life Depended on It."

"After the Flood, You Will Know Our True Names" quotes *The German Ideology* by Karl Marx.

Thanks

I am indebted to the poetic and political legacy of June Jordan; thank you for providing a north star. The following books served as inspiration in the drafting of this chapbook: *An Atlas of the Difficult World*, Adrienne Rich. *Look*, Solmaz Sharif. *Garments Against Women*, Anne Boyer. *Whereas*, Layli Long Soldier. *A Cruelty Special to Our Species*, Emily Jungmin Yoon. *A Theory of Birds,* Zaina Alsous. Thank you to these authors for their labor, rigor, and heart.

Sincere gratitude to Patrick Rosal for the encouragement and guidance and to Kary Wayson for her keen attention to these poems.

This book is dedicated to my family, friends, and comrades. I wrote it in honor of those who stewarded the land before us. It is for the artists, organizers, storytellers, and workers who resist injustice and demand a world of dignity and peace.

Marie Scarles is a writer, maker, and movement worker from the marshlands of Mystic, Connecticut. She received her MFA in Creative Writing from Rutgers University–Camden and is a graduate of Wesleyan University. Her work has appeared in *The Believer, Los Angeles Review of Books, The Rumpus, About Place Journal*, and elsewhere. She is the winner of the 2024 Quarterly West Poetry Prize. She lives and works in Brooklyn, New York, with her family.